Manifesting

Acquire the Knowledge to Actualize Your Ideal Existence
and Draw Abundance, Affection, Achievements, and
Profound Aspirations Through Optimistic Mental
Attitude

Lambert Seifert

TABLE OF CONTENT

Establish A Precise And Explicit Vision Whilst Directing Your Unwavering Efforts Towards The Realization Of Your Aspirations And Adherence To Your Core Values.

The majority of spiritual mystics hold the belief that in order to materialize one's aspirations and ambitions, it is essential to possess a lucid understanding of what they entail. It is imperative that you accurately ascertain their identity. It is crucial to articulate your aspirations and aspirations clearly, fostering unwavering conviction in their realization.

In our traditional lore, there exists a timeless adage which cautions individuals to exercise caution when articulating their desires, as they may ultimately find themselves confronted with the realization of those very aspirations. The formidable capabilities of your subconscious mind entail the ability to manifest your thoughts and emotions into tangible outcomes. You will attain what you desire. However, your cognitive faculties perceive any object of focus as a "wish" or "desire." Therefore, by directing your attention towards problems, obstacles, and difficulties, it is highly likely that these will dominate your experiences and continue to materialize in your external reality.

In order to actualize your true desires in life, it is imperative that you direct and concentrate all your energy towards them. Here are the clear and methodical steps that you can take to direct your attention towards your aspirations:

Ascertain the objectives or aspirations you hold

In order to actualize desired outcomes in one's life, it is vital to meticulously define and discern them. The majority of individuals commonly believe that they possess a genuine understanding of their desires; however, the reality is that this presumption is frequently unfounded. It is imperative that you take a moment to engage in introspection and carefully contemplate your true desires.

Initially, you will be prompted to identify items of material nature, such as a sizeable estate, a luxury handbag from Chanel, a BMW automobile, a highly compatible life partner, an exceptional child, a lucratively remunerative occupation, and substantial financial abundance. And as time goes on, you may eventually disclose something of a more personal nature, such as desiring to achieve a slimmer physique, aspire to greater attractiveness, yearn to explore the world, strive to be a more devoted spouse and parent, and long to dedicate more time to your family. Subsequently, delving further into this inquiry will expose the majority of your intrinsic aspirations and desires, such as the yearning for success, the longing to be admired, the desire for parental pride, the aspiration to amass wealth for altruistic purposes, and the yearning for respect from others.

One of the most effortless methods to actualize your desires is to direct your energy towards aspirations that align with your core principles. Matters of significance to you. The majority of individuals desire to possess pricey material possessions with the intention of garnering the esteem and admiration of their peers. The majority of individuals aspire to achieve affluence, primarily motivated by their desire to provide optimal living conditions for their families. Certain individuals aspire to achieve success in order to provide support and guidance to others.

After you have determined your values and appropriately identified your aspirations, proceed to document them. In order to actualize your desires, it is imperative to maintain clarity, and an effective method to accomplish this is to articulate your desires in written form. However, it is important to be precise when documenting your preferences and aspirations.

If your intention or objective is to "enter matrimony," clearly articulate the traits and qualities you desire in a prospective spouse. You are required to compile a comprehensive list of the qualities that you desire in a prospective life partner. Please be sure to provide a specific date as well.

The essence lies in being precise. Having a clear and precise articulation of your needs and aspirations can facilitate the universe's ability to manifest them.

Visualize

The act of visualizing holds paramount importance in the process of actualizing one's dreams and aspirations, as it brings forth lucidity and instills a sense of joy, fervor, and motivation. Dedicate a moment to envision yourself having achieved the aspirations you hold dear. Envision the sensations you experience when you are operating that ideal vehicle. Consider the emotions evoked by the experience of residing in your envisioned abode. Envision the profound sense of excitement that will engulf you upon securing the reservations for your global expedition.

Visualization is a technique that can be employed to bring about the realization of your aspirations. If you encounter difficulty in envisioning your aspirations, you can employ the technique of selecting images from magazines and incorporating them into either a dream journal or a visual display board. It is important to consistently refer to these images on a daily basis and endeavor to envision oneself having already accomplished the desired outcome. Envision possessing the Louis Vuitton handbag, the Gucci suit, the Rolex timepiece, or the BMW convertible. You must develop a sense for it. The sensation of possessing one's desired outcome will project favorable energies into the cosmos.

There existed an individual called Jessica, who held an enduring desire for a set of diamond earrings. She committed her aspiration to writing on a sheet of paper, demonstrating a remarkable level of precision. She expressed a desire for the heart-shaped diamond earrings, boasting a carat weight of 14. Throughout an extended period of time, spanning several days or even weeks, she consistently encounters individuals donning identical earrings or comes across said earrings within retail establishments. Lastly, she was taken aback when her spouse presented her with precisely the diamond earrings that she had envisioned several weeks prior.

The act of visualizing fosters positive energy and this positive energy serves as a catalyst for the occurrence of synchronicity, whereby the universe aligns the appropriate individuals, circumstances, and occurrences to manifest your aspirations.

The Recommendations And Methodologies Of The Law Of Attraction Requiring Your Implementation In Your Daily Life

Harnessing the principles of the Law of Attraction to manifest and sustain the life of your dreams does not have to be intricate. Sincerely. The primary concern among the majority of individuals pertains to harboring trust in the notion that it is as uncomplicated as it appears. Fundamentally, in order for the Law of Attraction to effectively assist you, it is essential for you to comprehend your desires, amplify them with a significant amount of positivity, and subsequently relinquish control (i.e. remove any obstacles hindering your progress). It is important to acknowledge that there are numerous individuals seeking methods to augment their manifestation endeavors - to commence attracting a greater abundance of relationships, opportunities, motivation, and happiness they aspire to acquire in their life.

Smoldering Desire

This is a vital admonition that if you do not master, the law of attraction simply cannot function in your life. This is a crucial instruction that should you fail to comprehend, the law of attraction will be rendered ineffective in your life. It is imperative to understand that without mastering this principle, the law of attraction will be incapable of operating in your life. It is imperative to possess a clear-cut objective, or perhaps even more favorable, an intense desire that is so significant and all-encompassing that it instills both exhilaration and trepidation within you simultaneously.

Do not allow yourself to become excessively concerned with the "How" for now.

It is not within your purview to possess complete knowledge from the outset. If you possess an objective, it must be specific, precisely defined, and you should possess a clear vision of the final outcome. Do not fret about the intricate details of how to achieve it at this stage. The way will appear to you.

Auto-recommendations & Affirmations

Automated suggestions constitute genuine recommendations. This represents the approaches through which we influence our subconscious mind, thereby manifesting all our desires in our lives. Create compelling statements and regularly review them.

Build Your Faith

Confidence, undoubtedly, holds the esteemed position of being the chief scientist of the brain. When your subconscious and confidence are unified, the vibrations are promptly interpreted by your subconscious mind and transmitted directly to the Universal Subconscious Mind, thus establishing a profound connection.

See It First-Visualize

Utilizing perceptions is indeed an exceptionally positive and remarkable method to prepare and prepare one's mind for the purpose of eliminating all negative thought patterns and replacing them with a successful, joyful, content, and prosperous pattern of thinking.

The Scientific Study Of Implementing Coordinated Measures

It is now appropriate to discuss initiating proactive measures. In the community centered around the Law of Attraction and manifestation, there is a notable prevalence of confusion among individuals, and such a result does not come as a surprise to us. Due to the fact that the information individuals receive originates directly from the spiritual realm and is exclusively intended for the spiritual realm, it is not appropriately deciphered and elucidated for those inhabiting the physical dimension. Consequently, numerous spirits become disoriented. They become entrapped in the state of anticipation for their manifestations, accelerate their impatience, and diminish their faith. We aim to prevent this undesirable outcome from happening to you.

Allow me to explain the process in detail:

In the realm of spirituality, the source of all spiritual teachings, manifestations can occur instantaneously. Nevertheless, in the realm of the corporeal, processes may require a certain amount of time. Simultaneously, the operational mechanisms on Earth serve to safeguard individuals from the deceptive influences that their cognitive faculties can impose upon them.

Envision the hypothetical scenario wherein you have the ability to contemplate an object of great value, such as a suitcase containing a million dollars, placed atop your kitchen table. Moreover, you possessed the ability to instantaneously manifest it solely through the power of your thoughts.

Simultaneously, you may consider a negative contemplation, such as the ingress of peculiar entities into your domicile, and materialize this vision. Instantly!

Indeed, we acknowledge that the aforementioned illustration might appear juvenile to a substantial number of individuals. And it is in accordance with commonly accepted principles. However, candidly speaking, the methods employed by individuals on Earth to engage in manifestation occasionally appear juvenile to us as well (we wish to avoid causing offense, but merely wish to offer guidance that will assist you in manifesting your desires effortlessly and joyfully!).

Every dimension abides by its own distinct set of regulations. The principles of spirituality remain constant, yet their manifestation on the material plane may exhibit slight variations. If you are perusing this text at present, it can be inferred that you possess both a spiritual and physical essence. Optimal outcomes in the act of manifestation can be achieved through the utilization of the contextual legal mechanisms pertaining to your immediate terrestrial environment. Integrate your material aspirations with the boundless potential of quantum energies. By harmonizing the pragmatic and transcendent aspects, you will experience significant accomplishments in your existence.

Rest assured that, according to our expertise, you will achieve remarkable accomplishments without succumbing to exhaustion. You will additionally alleviate yourself from numerous detrimental emotions, including uncertainty, animosity, and disillusionment.

Presumably, you are familiar with the concept of requesting, having faith, and subsequently obtaining what you desire, correct?

We have previously elucidated the essence of belief, therefore, allow us to promptly summarize: belief signifies a state of existence and a way of life.

Consequently, alternate expressions include: inquire, epitomize, and acquire.

You encapsulate the essence of something through a process of integration. You employ your complete range of capabilities- encompassing your cognitive processes, emotional states, and behavioral choices.

To illustrate this point, let us consider the case of Elena, who is currently embarking on a path towards achieving eminence as a renowned blogger. We previously informed you about the considerable difficulty we faced in enabling her to commence her path towards writing and disseminating her work. However, we understood that we could leverage her as a conduit on occasion. In all fairness, it should be noted that not all of her written content is derived directly from our organization. We highly commend her for her proficiency in acquiring knowledge, conducting research, and actively applying various self-help and spirituality principles, all of which greatly benefit her readers.

Previously, Elena exhibited a pattern of oscillating between polar opposites. As an illustration, she attempted to materialize success devoid of taking any proactive measures. She would become excessively engrossed in spiritual rituals and therapeutic practices. There is no inherent issue with engaging in spiritual rituals and healing practices; it is strongly advised that you adhere to whichever methods prove beneficial for you.

The problem? She became excessively engrossed in matters pertaining to spirituality and the esoteric, consequently impeding her capacity to maintain practicality and sound judgement, and hindered her propensity to pursue decisive actions and progress.

She even entertained the notion of offering her services without charge and generously dispensing all her earnings, which ultimately resulted in an unfavorable financial predicament.

However, she also encountered an additional extreme. She embarked on an online entrepreneurial venture and became excessively engrossed in the demanding nature of the endeavor. She desired to compensate for embracing a rather unconventional and solely pragmatic approach, lacking any regards for spiritual harmony. Therefore, she became overwhelmed with exhaustion and experienced a lack of contentment.

Throughout that period, she endured a considerable amount of adversity, as her ability to attain monetary prosperity proved to be transient, leading to persistent apprehension regarding the potential loss of her savings and diligent efforts.

Fortunately, she awakened at the opportune moment and resolved to heed her celestial guides of manifestation. At a later juncture, she theorized: a realization emerged that the term "attraction" harbors the fundamental presence of "action".

Following a detailed examination of individuals who have attained comprehensive success through the practice of the Law of Attraction (LOA) and the art of manifesting, including renowned LOA experts like Bob Proctor and Rhonda Byrne, in addition to ordinary individuals who lead remarkable lives as a result of applying the principles of LOA, she eventually came to the realization that equilibrium is imperative. To gain insight into your true self, maintain a profound connection with the Source, and continually experience a sense of guidance, it is necessary to engage in inner introspection and cultivate energetic practices. Additionally, it is imperative to engage in regular and structured physical exertion in order to maintain stability and make progress.

There is no definitive guideline for establishing equilibrium between action and attraction. We strongly encourage you to engage in practicing and independently explore in order to gain proficiency.

However, in the majority of instances, it is imperative that both are required.

Presently, for the purpose of clarification, let us articulate: in the majority of instances.

Since it is undeniably feasible to materialize spontaneously, and such occurrences take place. Certain manifestations may not necessitate any course of action. We strongly urge you to have faith in the existence of magic. However, yet again, to have faith implies embodying and embracing existence. Therefore, embrace the enchantment and embody the extraordinary. Do your part. Do your thing.

Nevertheless, in relation to achieving success, fostering creativity, attaining financial stability, as well as ensuring good health and fitness, it is advised that you reinforce your spiritual and energetic endeavors by engaging in resolute, harmonious actions that resonate with your inner being.

Therefore, a few months ago, we made the decision to encourage Elena's initiation of a blog. Initially, she encountered significant opposition due to her previous adverse encounters in website development. Her acquaintances in the business industry would often impart to her that engaging in blogging was entirely unproductive.

Through the application of the Law of Attraction, she was able to alter her cognitive patterns. She would envision herself in the year ahead, managing a prosperous blog. She had envisioned receiving emails from satisfied readers.

She proceeded to act based on that optimistic standpoint. The process of establishing the blog and generating the initial posts proceeded exceptionally well. Despite her lack of technical expertise. There was no stress. She derived immense satisfaction from each and every instance of what her peers would typically categorize as arduous labor.

Now, she continues to diligently pursue aligned efforts on a daily basis. Despite the task involving the creation of a preliminary version for a blog post. That is her established guideline! Regardless of life's demands, she remains unwaveringly dedicated to maintaining her blog. Allocating 15 minutes per day yields greater benefits than abstaining entirely.

Why? Well, due to her belief in the concept of the compound effect.

You achieve observable outcomes through the consistent implementation of incremental actions on a daily basis.

Elena applies the identical principle for her self-improvement and spiritual endeavors. She has a strong affinity for engaging in meditation and the practice of tapping on a regular basis. Despite the potential demands of life, she remains committed to doing it as it brings her a sense of gratification. Furthermore, it is important to note that dedicating five minutes per day consistently is more beneficial than not doing anything at all.

Moreover, within the context of the spiritual realm, the concept of time, specifically in a linear fashion, does not exist. The key focus in this context is to ensure that you consistently maintain alignment with your vision on a daily basis, by gradually taking incremental steps towards your desired objective.

You proceed with composure, stepping forward gracefully.

There is no necessity to rush, toil excessively, or exhaust oneself.

Indeed, it is possible to reduce your working hours while enhancing the quality, concentration, tranquility, and efficiency of the hours allocated to working.

Due to the significance of the energy from which you derive your actions.

Additionally, we would like to emphasize that individuals possess varying preferences and inclinations. We are not implying that you should mimic or emulate Elena's actions.

She inquired about her course, received her solutions, internalized them, and quietly labored in the background due to her unwavering belief.

In a manner similar to how the intricate workings of the Universe operate unbeknownst to us, lending their support (as do your esteemed Manifestation Angels), it is within your capability to contribute by adhering to your purpose, engaging in diligent and discreet labor, and adopting the potency of unobtrusive, yet unwavering effort. All of this while embodying the essence of abundance, serenity, and self-assurance.

Naturally, we comprehend that certain days may present some difficulties. Elena was taken aback when her blog experienced a disruption due to certain technical complications. However, she swiftly regained her composure and collected her thoughts. She envisioned her website functioning normally, subsequently contacting her hosting company and experiencing prompt resolution of the issue.

We strongly advise engaging in the comprehensive exploration of the Law of

Attraction alongside diverse methodologies, including affirmations, scripting, and visualizations. Elena has excelled in authoring a plethora of books that provide comprehensive guidance.

However, it is important to bear in mind that individuals vary significantly from one another. Certain individuals have a predisposition towards affirmation, others are inclined towards scripting, and there are those who find solace in visualization. Certain individuals derive great pleasure from concocting their own distinctive blend of manifestation techniques.

Allocate sufficient time and physical distance to engage in learning and experimentation. However, once you have discovered a methodology that is effective for you and aligns with your calling, it is advisable to wholeheartedly pursue it. Do it every day.

The Mechanics Of Abundance Checks

The practice of utilizing abundance checks as a manifestation tool has been present for a considerable length of time, yet it gained wider recognition due to its portrayal in the documentary, The Secret.

In earlier times, bank checks were non-existent, thus individuals resorted to inscribing their financial transactions on a scroll or parchment paper, which they carried along.

The practice of writing abundance checks is effective because it serves as a tangible embodiment of the abundance one wishes to manifest.

Typically, when one strives to materialize something within the realm of the tangible, they primarily engage with concepts, notions, and imaginative constructs.

However, when employing abundance checks, one is already witnessing the physical manifestation right before their own eyes.

The fundamental reason behind the effectiveness of this manifestation technique lies in the tangible presence of a physical document, symbolizing your manifestation in the physical realm.

Consider this alternative phrasing in a more formal tone: "Furthermore, due to its inherent physicality, its energy possesses greater potency and lends itself more readily to attunement, facilitating the manifestation of one's aspirations."

One additional rationale for the effectiveness of utilizing abundance checks as a manifestation technique lies in its incorporation of all the requisite components for the successful execution of any manifestation or law of attraction endeavor.

Inquire: When completing those checks, you are distinctly and explicitly requesting what you desire without any ambiguity.

It is imperative to acknowledge that a lack of clarity or specificity regarding one's desires significantly hampers the process of manifestation.

When issuing an abundance check, you demonstrate meticulous precision in determining the precise amount you desire. You effectively communicate your intentions, facilitating a harmonious alignment with the universe that expedites the fulfillment of your aspirations.

Have faith: Completion of an abundance check also signifies belief. By endorsing that check to yourself, you have symbolically demonstrated your belief in deserving that precise sum, and it is expected that the cosmos will align to manifest it for you.

Imitate or assume the role of: Completing an abundance check can also be regarded as simulating or assuming the role of. It is unlikely that you currently possess gainful employment, a contractual agreement, or personal connections capable of providing you with a $10 million monetary sum at present. However, when you proceed to issue a written check in your own name, you are effectively conveying to the cosmos your undeniable worthiness and genuine desire for such a reward.

You are expressing to the universe, 'There exist individuals who receive such remittances on a consistent basis, and I aspire to join their ranks as well'.

Upon receipt: Subsequent to the act of writing the check, you are required to bear it in your possession, further exemplifying your anticipation through this symbolic gesture. This demonstrates your faith in attaining your desired outcome.

In actuality, one would not haphazardly toss a $10 million dollar check without regard. Until the check is duly cashed, it would be handled with great caution and safeguarded fervently.

By keeping your abundance check in your possession, you are exhibiting unwavering faith and conviction in the aforementioned procedure. You are demonstrating a sense of anticipation to the universe. You are channeling a greater amount of positive energy towards your manifestations, thereby significantly expediting the pace at which you will attain your desired outcomes.

While the primary purpose of abundance checks is often to magnetize wealth, their utility extends beyond monetary means. This is a surplus check rather than a currency check, thus it is intended not only for materializing wealth but also for bringing about abundance in any aspect that holds significance to you.

One may utilize it to earnestly request the universe for any desire, be it optimal well-being, an amorous companion, a residence, an automobile, gainful employment, or any other coveted aspiration.

Does it Work?

I successfully attained a sum of $200 within a span of 4 to 5 days during my initial attempt, and on my second endeavor, I was able to manifest an amount exceeding $2000.

I expeditiously informed both my spouse and offspring, imparting to them the necessary knowledge and skills for its use. Both individuals attained favorable outcomes upon their initial attempt as well. My daughter's expressions of behaviors occurred with greater expedition than my own.

I initiated the instruction of this methodology to my clients and incorporated it into my own practice on a more frequent basis. On a monthly basis, I issue a self-directed remittance for a predetermined amount that corresponds to the desired income for my business in that particular month, a practice which frequently proves successful.

On occasion, I am able to acquire an even larger quantity/variation.

I have received numerous testimonies from several clients, which has greatly influenced my decision to author this book. One of the key motivations behind my choice is the prevailing misconception and limited awareness surrounding this manifestation technique among the general public.

It is anticipated that a greater number of individuals will become acquainted with the practice of utilizing abundance checks as a means to manifest their elevated states of being.

How does the manifestation of abundance occur through the use of the abundance check?

This is a frequently asked question.

Frequently, individuals inquire as to whether funds will spontaneously manifest in their account at a future time.

Regrettably, that is not the case.

The actions undertaken by the universe serve to create avenues through which you may encounter opportunities, establish connections, receive job offers, foster friendships, acquire gifts, or even experience lottery winnings, all contingent upon the intentions and desires you have expressed through various means.

Consider the case of Jim Carrey as an example. Through a sequence of events orchestrated by fate, he was granted a few minor acting opportunities which eventually led to a significant role. Subsequently, this major role served as a catalyst, paving the way for him to secure a highly lucrative film role that ultimately accrued him a substantial sum of $10 million dollars.

Therefore, if you happen to be inquisitive about the subsequent outcomes following the completion of your act of writing an abundance check, the aforementioned statement should provide you with a sense of clarification.

At times, when endeavoring to actualize minor occurrences such as acquiring $200 or receiving a complimentary meal, such manifestations can transpire with greater expeditiousness. A friend could potentially reach out to invite you for a lunch outing or extend financial support to you by means of a gift.

There are a multitude of potential manifestations for your desires.

You could potentially encounter a timely business prospect that could expedite your financial gains.

The possibility exists that the universe may influence someone to generously offer you monetary assistance or orchestrate a fortuitous encounter with an individual who possesses the necessary connections and guidance to support the realization of your aspirations.

It is imperative to maintain awareness, exercise patience, and uphold a positive mindset throughout the entirety of the process until one achieves their desires.

Please refrain from entertaining the notion that the efficacy of abundance checks is negated in any way. Many significant events or activities could be occurring behind the scenes, unbeknownst to you.

It is imperative to maintain a positive outlook and cultivate patience.

When making an order at a restaurant, it is not customary to continuously inquire about its progress from the waiter.

It is not necessary to oversee the activities of the chef to ensure that he is preparing your food appropriately.

You just make your order and wait patiently because you know that that you'll get your food.

The universe possesses a level of power and capability that far surpasses what we typically acknowledge.

It has the potential to fulfill your aspirations; therefore, refrain from exacerbating matters by displaying impatience, anxiety, or succumbing to doubt and restrictive convictions.

Up to this point in the initial chapter, we have elucidated the concepts of silence, cognitive fallacies, as well as the distinction between phenomenal and non-phenomenal existence. We trust that you have derived interest from this dialogue; nonetheless, please be aware that all the information presented thus far is purely theoretical in nature. It has served as nourishment for your intellect. Concepts are an essential component of human nature. As human beings, we are inherently social entities that rely on abstract notions in order to effectively engage in communication and share thoughts and perspectives. For this objective, concepts hold significant value.

The aforementioned statement applies equally to the realm of cognition. The prowess of our intellect is integral to our triumph in the process of evolution. The primary driver of our species' prevalence is derived from our exceptional capacity to resolve challenges. The detriment to our species lies in our tendency to align ourselves with our cognitive faculties. We hold the conviction that our identities fundamentally consist of our intellect and physical form.

The manifestation of our sense of detachment, brought about by our association with our intellect and physical form, has led to our behavior driven by anxiety, specifically the anxiety surrounding insufficient resources and the anxiety of relinquishment. It is within this framework that all our difficulties arise, whether they pertain to the individual or the collective domain. Moreover, it restricts our capacity to attain heightened states of cognition and perception.

Envision a thespian who is engaged in a theatrical performance. This actor possesses a profound sense of identification with her character, thereby flawlessly portraying the character to the audience. Once the play concludes, she proceeds to remove her make-up, change her attire, and departs for her residence. The actor has ceased to portray her character. She is currently transitioning into the roles of a spouse, a parent, a friend, or a daughter. She has the potential to engage in social gatherings with acquaintances, embark on outdoor recreational activities such as camping, or partake in romantic encounters. The actor's capabilities beyond the stage are exceedingly vast.

When we associate ourselves with the mind or body, we resemble the performer who persistently regards herself as the role she portrayed even after the conclusion of the performance. It is imperative that we acquire the ability to surpass cognitive limitations and explore the inherent depths and profound facets of our being. Meditation is deemed to be one of the most formidable techniques for achieving this objective. The essence of meditation lies in the restoration of tranquility. It discerns the mirages inherent in the fabric of existence and facilitates our access to the metaphysical plane.

Daily Exercise:

When acquiring the skill of meditation, it is important to bear in mind several crucial aspects.

Preserve a mindset characterized by complete acceptance and impartiality towards every encounter you undergo.

Do not attempt to exert dominance, alter, or oppose any aspect of your perceived reality.

Grant unfettered autonomy for every facet of your experience to manifest in its entirety.

During the process of meditation, one might encounter various thoughts, including:

I find that my thoughts persist unrelentingly, exhibiting no signs of deceleration.

This is too difficult.

This is boring.

I have more pressing matters to attend to.

This is not working.

Is my approach in accordance with the correct methodology?

Disregard these thoughts and persist in directing your attention towards the practice of meditation.

Finally, there is no correct way or incorrect way to meditate as long as you are allowing yourself to be a witness to all of your experiences.

Please assume a relaxed posture, gently close your eyes, and breathe at a steady pace.

Direct your attention to your breath, concentrating on the sensations as it moves in and out of your body.

While maintaining your attention on your breathing, you will observe the emergence of thoughts. When they manifest, kindly disregard their presence and redirect your focus towards your breath.

By maintaining your attention on your breath, you will eventually reach a stage where you can effortlessly sustain your awareness of it. Once you have entered this stage, permit yourself to observe and bear witness to everything that emerges within your consciousness.

Observe the manner in which thoughts, sensations, and perceptions manifest within your consciousness and subsequently diminish. These cognitive occurrences manifest and vanish within the realm of your consciousness. Nevertheless, the state of awareness remains consistent and immutable.

The subjective experiences one encounters can be characterized as either positive, neutral, or negative; however, it is important to note that awareness itself remains unaffected by these qualities.

As the significance attributed to the observation of mental phenomena diminishes, their vitality will wane, leading to a state of tranquility within your mind. It is even conceivable that you might encounter intervals characterized by serenity and expansiveness. Should you choose to do so, it is important to recognize that tranquility and emptiness are likewise cognitive occurrences. Avoid developing emotional attachment to any experience; instead, maintain the role of an observer.

Please feel free to engage in meditation for as long as you see fit.

Embrace Self-Centeredness In Order To Truly Serve Others

However, it is important to bear in mind that excessive selflessness holds no superior virtue or nobility compared to excessive selfishness. Both are errors according to Wallace D. Wattles

Each one of us is a distinct individual possessing a unique array of talents and capabilities. Regrettably, a significant portion of individuals fail to adequately harness and realize their talents, thus falling short of reaching their full potential. Clearly, one cannot anticipate acquiring excellence by promoting averageness. In order to achieve our objectives and aspirations in life, it is imperative for us to employ these capabilities. In order for such an outcome to occur, we must prioritize our individual needs foremost. In order to ultimately serve the interests of others and engage in altruistic acts, it is imperative that we first embrace a certain level of self-interest. Doesn't appear to be correct, does it? Let's explain:

The Benefits and Strategies of Embracing Self-Care

You will be unable to attain your objectives and materialize your authentic aspirations should you allow your life to be governed by external influences. To fully manifest your aspirations, it is necessary to allocate dedicated periods of time solely devoted to personal growth and pursuits. The deliberations presented throughout this entire book hold no practical value if one fails to allocate due attention to their own wants, needs, and strategies for fulfilling their aspirations. It is essential to prioritize your own well-being and properly allocate your resources of care, love, and attention to yourself before extending them to others.

And unless you develop sufficient self-interest to prioritize such actions, you will never attain the desired personal transformation, nor will you achieve a level of influence where you can effectively contribute to the welfare of others. For example, should you lack a state of good health, you will perpetually remain incapable of assisting others in achieving wellness. One cannot effectively contribute to the improvement of others' well-being if they are unwell themselves; they would be incapable of providing any significant assistance, wouldn't they? It is evident from this example that a foremost endeavour should be to prioritize personal growth, thereby enabling one to reach a stage where one can have a transformative impact on the lives of others.

Just Say No

Do you possess the tendency to rarely decline any requests made of you, even if it necessitates making personal sacrifices? It is highly probable that if you are perusing this book, you are indeed the intended audience. This is not a matter of disgrace, but it certainly requires attention. You are unable to make any enhancements to yourself until you divert the necessary focus towards your own well-being. By acquiescing to the desires and demands of others without discretion, you are inherently denying yourself the opportunity to prioritize your own needs and aspirations. Acquire the skill of declining. The subsequent occasion individuals make requests that demand a significant amount of your time, energy, or financial resources, simply reject their proposals. Over time, you will notice a decrease in the number of inquiries being made.

Ensure your personal well-being

Devote effort towards devising a selection of strategies to prioritize self-care and nurture one's well-being. While some suggestions may appear self-evident, presented below are a selection of ideas that one may choose to incorporate:

Physical activity. Prioritizing self-care should be at the forefront of your personal agenda. As the popular saying goes, if one's health is compromised, one's possession of anything else becomes inconsequential. And they are right. Initiate the practice of allocating designated time for physical activity, even if it entails dedicating as little as 15 minutes per week. You shall observe an augmentation in your energy levels, alongside an enhancement in your cognitive function, attributed to the augmented circulation of blood to your brain.

Ensure proper nutrition. This implies a more comprehensive approach to nutrition. It is essential to ensure that your body receives the necessary nutrients and sustenance, while concurrently finding pleasure in the consumption of food. Engage in the process of acquiring culinary skills to prepare the dishes that truly bring you satisfaction. It is crucial to engage fully in the act of consuming meals, regardless of whether you have prepared them yourself or not. Eliminate any sources of distraction and direct your primary attention towards the act of consuming your meal. Please endeavor to abstain from watching the television or diverting your attention to anything other than your meal. You will discover that not only will you derive greater pleasure from your meals, but you will also consume them at a more gradual pace, leading to improved digestion.

Please take pleasure in. Dedicate a small portion of your daily routine to engaging in activities that bring you joy and satisfaction. Whether it is engaging in guitar playing, dedicating time to painting, indulging in music listening, practicing woodworking or pottery, or even undertaking meditation, among other activities. Allow your inner essence to shine unhindered. It is not necessary for the duration to be prolonged. It may require only a short duration of 30 minutes. Frequently within our society, we find ourselves excessively engrossed in both our professional endeavors and social engagements, neglecting to allocate any time for self-care and personal fulfillment. Such a disposition is detrimental to our well-being, as numerous individuals would attest. It precludes opportunities for imaginative self-expression and the derived pleasure. Our society bestows esteem and veneration upon individuals who dedicate themselves to toiling for 80 hours a week, but one must question the associated sacrifice. It does not justify the value. Take time for yourself.

Please participate. Devoting time to our loved ones and cultivating meaningful connections should always remain at the forefront of our priorities, regardless of the demands of our professions, aspirations, or excessively laborious work schedules. We are striving to cultivate these very connections in order to ultimately derive enjoyment from them. Being an introvert is acceptable, just like being an extrovert, however, even introverts have their own interpersonal connections. The sole means by which we can nourish the relationships we hold dear and desire to maintain is to actively participate in them. Otherwise, they go away. It is an embodiment of the Law in action, yet again. By investing time in a relationship, one is bound to encounter an increased abundance of it.

Enlargen. The world is big. REALLY big. There is a plethora of sights and discoveries to be made. It is highly probable that you entertain a certain degree of inclination towards visiting a certain location, be it a secluded meteorological facility in Antarctica or a diminutive tropical isle in the Pacific. Make it happen. The longing stems from the innate yearning of your essence for manifestation. Pursue this for your own benefit, and remain undeterred by factors such as time and financial constraints.

Try these guidelines. These are merely a handful of suggestions to aid you in initiating personal growth and development. Selflessness and prioritizing others over oneself are attributes that are greatly idealized and lauded within our society. For individuals whose sense of self-value is not exceptionally high, this phenomenon can exert a particularly captivating allure, and it is frequently these individuals whom our society exploits for its own benefit. It is imperative to achieve equilibrium. The whole point of this conversation on being "selfish" in this case is in fact to be be selfless, ultimately; but always beware the extremes of either, they are deadly to your health, wealth, and happiness.

Step Three: Transfer It onto a Board.

A vision board is essentially a graphical compilation, sketch, or assemblage designed to facilitate the manifestation of enduring aspirations and objectives. Vision boards serve as a meticulously curated medium for individuals to gather and preserve significant life experiences, functioning as a symbolic representation of their aspirations - commonly referred to as a "dream board." In general, a vision board typically comprises a multitude of images that symbolize significant milestones in an individual's life, alongside imaginative depictions sourced from magazines and online platforms that provoke inspiration or evoke profound emotions. These images encompass a plethora of possibilities, spanning from a cherished family photograph or a memorable snapshot from a vacation, to portrayals of inspiring individuals that serve as symbols of your aspirations or significant milestones on the path towards achieving a specific objective.

Individuals each construct a personal vision board by drawing from the experiences that have most profoundly shaped their lives. You have the option to utilize a blackboard, calendar, or note cards for the creation of your vision board – the choice is entirely yours, and it serves as a platform for unleashing your artistic flair. After acquiring all necessary resources, one may commence the process of creating visual depictions illustrating the envisioned elements of their ideal life, including events, accomplishments, and tangible possessions. One can commence by documenting everything from the instance one acquired knowledge of their ideals – including any realizations experienced during the visualization process - and culminate the board with uplifting quotes or reflections that strengthen the envisioned outcome. Consider a broader spectrum of factors beyond your current sources of motivation. What would you consider as content that will uplift your spirits and inspire you on occasions when you experience a lack of motivation or moments of negativity? What will serve as a source of renewed motivation for you, or alternatively, what will provide you with the necessary impetus to maintain a strong level of discipline?

One may also make use of magazines, newspapers, calendars, or any alternative medium containing visual representations. An inherent benefit associated with the utilization of these visual prompts resides in their effortless setup in one's residence or any location believed to assist individuals in their pursuit. One other notable advantage of employing a vision board is the ability to modify the visual representations at will. Should you perceive a shift or evolution in your vision or purpose, you have the capability to substitute particular elements with those that align more effectively with the updated objectives. This will help ensure that your visualization process and manifestation journey remain dynamic and stimulating.

When constructing a vision board, it may be beneficial to incorporate notable milestones that have transpired throughout your life. By engaging in this practice, you can effectively conceptualize the strides you have achieved up until this point. Subsequently, it can bolster your determination to persist in pursuing your envisioned aspirations and precisely identify the modifications you ought to undertake each day to manifest your desired lifestyle. Utilizing visual representations that symbolize the favorable facets of your life and significant milestones that have contributed to your progress can be advantageous. This approach serves as a source of motivation, particularly as it instills a sense of pride when one reflects upon the considerable distance they have covered.

If you feel that you haven't really made any progress in any of the areas of your life that you have set for yourself, simply take a look at your vision board and see what improvements you could make on a daily basis. To what extent have you progressed? How many of the objectives depicted on your vision board have been realized? If you encounter challenges in attaining these ideals, it may be beneficial to take note of certain factors that you believe may underlie this issue. You may also consider incorporating a daily regimen of actionable steps in order to break free from this cycle of stagnation. By employing this approach, you will enhance your ability to mentally perceive your objectives with a similar sense of tangibility, and the more diligently you adhere to your strategic course of action, the greater progress you will make towards attaining them. By envisioning your objectives as imminent realities, you will ignite a sense of motivation within yourself, propelling you to diligently strive towards their attainment. Furthermore, your board will function as a conduit for incessant introspection, enabling you to vigilantly contemplate your thoughts, emotions, and their potential impact on your quest for manifestation.

Indeed, vision boards prove to be an excellent resource for eliciting a sense of optimism within oneself By employing these tools, one has the ability to cultivate personal inspiration and enhance one's emotional state, as contemplating the compelling aspirations we strive for generally brings great joy. It is imperative to bear in mind that when utilizing a vision board to symbolize one's life purpose, it is essential to ensure the accurate portrayal of said purpose.

Strategies For Cultivating A Constructive Mental Outlook

You may be familiar with the notion of describing someone as either pessimistic or optimistic. The reality is that we possess the option to determine whether we desire to adopt a positive mindset. It does not arise from innate abilities. You possess the utmost capability to alter your mindset. When you commit to this change, it could lead you to a more successful, happier life.

These guidelines will assist you in initiating your quest for a more optimistic perspective.

Act More Positive

When an individual, regardless of whether they are merely feigning, exhibits the demeanor of a positive individual, it can exert an influence on their mindset, leading to a gradual transformation into a genuinely positive person. Research has indicated that the act of intentionally smiling can potentially alter one's emotional state. Moreover, by displaying a demeanor of assurance, one has the potential to positively impact their self-assurance.

When encountering an unfamiliar individual, make an effort to abstain from employing any adverse descriptive terms. Present yourself as if you are experiencing the pinnacle of joy, and demonstrate affability through engaging in conversations with those around you. In the comfort of your own residence, endeavor to encircle yourself with objects of motivation and images that exude positivity, thus imbuing within yourself a sense of inspiration and contentment.

Be More Appreciative

If one were to allocate a mere five minutes to fostering gratitude in one's existence, it could potentially lead to transformative shifts in one's outlook. Ensure that you have a notepad readily available for this exercise. Subsequently, document the occurrences throughout the day that you hold in high regard. You are welcome to document anything that has brought you joy with regards to your current surroundings.

It is possible that you recall a significant conversation you had with a relative. It is plausible that a captivating butterfly might have been accompanying you during your morning stroll. You have been granted the salary increase you requested. This activity may seem straightforward, however, it carries significant implications in terms of altering one's emotional state.

Direct your attention to the current events/ occurrences.

Numerous individuals with a pessimistic outlook have a tendency to reside in the past while simultaneously fixating on their future. They persistently ruminate on regrets stemming from their past and exhibit concerns regarding the resolution of their newfound difficulties.

The primary determinant for cultivating a positive mental outlook is to maintain unwavering concentration on the current moment. Grant yourself the opportunity to fully embrace and appreciate every intricate aspect of your extraordinary existence. Once you initiate this practice, you will find it increasingly effortless to derive satisfaction from simple sources, such as expressing tenderness to a pet, embarking on a tranquil stroll amidst the natural environment, or luxuriating in the comforting embrace of cool bed linens.

Certain individuals discover that the practice of mindfulness exercises serves as an effective means to enhance their capacity for reveling in the current moment. To initiate the process, allocate a specific duration during which one can engage in mindfulness exercises by allocating mental space and directing attention solely towards controlled breathing.

Uncover Positive Influences

It can present a challenge to maintain a positive outlook when one finds themselves amidst individuals who consistently perceive the negative aspects, express criticism, and engage in continuous complaint. These attitudes are highly contagious, and individuals who consistently harbor such a mindset may deride your attempts to foster a positive outlook.

Due to this factor, it is crucial to exercise discernment while selecting companions, and prioritize associating with individuals who exhibit supportiveness, optimism, and dynamism. Engaging in social interactions with these individuals will invigorate your spirit and provide ample opportunities for appreciation.

Avoid consistently succumbing to a pessimistic outlook.

Regardless of your aspirations in life, it is important to envision yourself successfully attaining your objectives. Do not permit yourself to entertain thoughts of perplexity, fear, humiliation, or defeat. Instead of constructing excessively intricate depictions of pleasure, success, and happiness, a beneficial approach to diminish your inclination to consistently perceive the negative is to consistently reinforce your belief in your ability to conquer any challenge that may confront you. Through diligent dedication and the passage of time, one has the capacity to transform any melancholic, burdensome, or arduous circumstance into a constructive encounter, thereby fortifying oneself for future accomplishments.

Spread positivity among your peers Encourage a positive atmosphere among those in your vicinity Promote an optimistic outlook among those you interact with Inspire those around you with positive vibes

Transmitting joy to others is an additional stride in the direction of fostering a constructive mindset. When one demonstrates kindness towards others, the reciprocation they receive creates a feedback loop that generates a heightened sense of positivity within oneself. Subsequently, this will foster an inclination within you to disseminate your positivity among others.

There is no necessity for you to undertake any significant measures to incorporate this into your daily existence. Simply ensure that you offer compliments to individuals whenever they merit it. It is advisable to express appreciation to your cousin by complimenting her appearance in her new dress, extend gratitude to your boss for the additional assistance provided on the project, recall a reason that contributed to your affection towards your partner, or offer congratulations to a colleague for delivering an exceptional presentation.

All of these actions will contribute to enhancing the well-being of others, while also aiding you in attaining your objective of cultivating a more optimistic demeanor.

Practice Self-Care Effectively

It is essential to understand that spreading positivity to others does not necessitate the complete allocation of all one's resources towards selfless endeavors. Achieving success and happiness necessitates a dedication to fulfilling one's necessities.

It is exceedingly challenging to maintain a positive outlook in situations where one's energy and vitality have been completely depleted. One should never experience feelings of guilt when declining invitations, especially when the purpose is to prioritize self-care and rejuvenation.

Ensure that every day of your existence entails a single instance of an arbitrary benevolent deed directed towards oneself. It could entail indulging in a late morning slumber, revisiting the pages of your cherished literature, immersing in the melody of your preferred composition, or preparing a nutritious culinary delight. Recognizing one's inherent worthiness of care and affection constitutes a significant aspect of cultivating a positive mindset.

Utilize The Technique Of Visual Representation To Chart Your Progressive Actions.

When executed correctly, the act of envisioning your significant life objectives can serve as a driving force for inspiration. There is no doubt about it. One can perceive the aroma of accomplishment and even experience its flavor. That is a reflection of its authenticity. One cannot help but experience heightened emotional arousal. You have a clear visual representation of how you would appear. You possess a certain aura that garners respect and attracts others towards your presence. You also experience the profound sense of fulfillment derived from leading a rich and purposeful existence.

This section marks the juncture at which one experiences a sense of fulfillment and reaches the pinnacle of their performance. It is not unexpected that you are entirely involved on an emotional level. Do not squander this opportunity.

It is essential to comprehend that there exists a significant distinction between visualization and daydreaming, namely that the former serves as a means to establish a connection between your present circumstances and your desired destination.

Conversely, indulging in daydreams entails experiencing emotional catharsis through envisioning oneself liberated from present challenges. It resembles an incarcerated individual indulging in fantasies of liberation—an existence where one possesses a dwelling, pursues a career, savors an exhilarating nocturnal social life, and freely indulges in personal desires. Through the act of envisioning himself in a distant location, leading a life vastly dissimilar to his present circumstances, he endeavours to mitigate the severity of his imprisonment.

Engaging in imaginative musings promptly evokes a profound emotional response. Here's the problem. When engaging in daydreaming, the primary objective is to alleviate the distress caused by present frustrations. Regard it as a form of psychological and intellectual sedative or analgesic. You experience a poignant surge of emotions that serves to alleviate the distress of your everyday life. What is your projection for the subsequent events?

Engaging in idle fantasies does not contribute to the resolution of your circumstances. You are currently residing in a confined space. You're still feeling stuck. It appears that there will be no imminent alteration in the current situation. Consequently, one finds themselves perpetuating the identical patterns that initially ensnared them.

When engaging in the act of daydreaming, one is able to attain a rapid means of escaping reality, thereby facilitating the continuation and intensification of their fantasies. You persist in perpetuating this procedure, which evokes a sense of gratification; however, no discernible alterations occur on a daily basis.

This scenario is distinctly dissimilar to envisioning the desired destination. When one employs visualization techniques and embraces genuine emotional involvement, the desire is to embody that individual. You envision yourself embodying that individual. You get a roadmap. What steps must you take in order to transition from your current position to your desired destination? The most advantageous aspect of this situation is that the roadmap is essentially self-generated, as it simply entails retracing your steps.

As previously indicated in the preceding discourse, when one fosters a sense of high motivation towards the ultimate realization of their significant aspiration, it becomes more feasible to closely examine the intricacies and procedures that contributed to its achievement. Commence by identifying your objective and work in reverse. The greater the extent to which one envisions oneself experiencing the desired lifestyle, the more evident the particulars become. You begin to perceive the disparities, and subsequently proceed to address them.

Exercising Utmost Mastery Over The Law Of Attraction In Your Existence And Actualizing Your Aspired Reality

The principle of attraction operates within your life regardless of your desires, and whether you possess consciousness of its presence. To manifest your wants and desires, you have to use the law of attraction to manifest all the things that you want and desire.

Below are the prescribed actions that one could undertake in order to achieve thorough mastery over the law of attraction:

Censor your thoughts. Allocate a suitable amount of time to cultivate mindfulness and attunement towards the contents of your thoughts. It is essential to direct your attention towards desired outcomes rather than dwelling on undesired ones.

Whenever you find yourself engaged in negative thinking, expeditiously substitute it with a constructive or optimistic thought.

Engage in visualization exercises during your commute to work using public transportation. Additionally, you have the option to engage in visualization exercises during the period of time before your scheduled appointment with the doctor, or immediately upon awakening each morning.

Each and every thought and utterance is regarded as an act of prayer. Each thought and utterance comprises an authoritative directive. You have to make sure that your words and your thoughts are aligned with your dreams and desires.

To effectively govern the principles of the law of attraction in your life, it is imperative that you exert dominion over your emotions. To effectively materialize one's aspirations and objectives, it is imperative to emanate affirmative energies. You are obliged to bring blessings upon those acquainted with you.

In order to materialize your desired outcomes in life, it is imperative to assume the demeanor or mannerisms that align with those goals. One must experience a sense of having been bestowed with their individual "preferences" and "longings."

Practice gratitude regularly. Appreciation is a potent emotion that has the ability to attract positive outcomes into one's life. The greater your sense of gratitude, the more likely you are to draw positive occurrences, individuals, and situations into your life.

Do Not Dwell Upon Dreams Of The Future, But Rather Embrace The Present Moment And Derive Pleasure From It.

The implementation of manifestation as a technique can yield favorable outcomes when executed with proficiency. A prevalent belief among numerous individuals is that envisioning acquiring every material possession will result in their effortless acquisition. Furthermore, I have also made attempts at employing manifestation techniques in order to attain success and prosperity in my life, and in doing so, I have come to the realization that simply envisioning or fantasizing about desired outcomes does not suffice to achieve successful manifestation. Many individuals frequently envision acquiring various aspects of a fulfilled life, such as a lavish automobile, spacious residence, or an attractive romantic partner. However, they often find themselves engrossed in these fantasies rather than living in accordance with the actualities of their existence. When we envision acquiring something in our future, it perpetually remains in the realm of the future, eluding our grasp indefinitely. In this scenario, we emerge as the principal barrier in attaining our desired objectives in life. Engaging in constructive imagination is beneficial, yet indulging in idle daydreams does not serve as the optimal method for bringing desires into reality. Whenever we engage in imaginative contemplation and conceive the notion that in the forthcoming months, we shall possess an opulent automobile, our Subconscious mind proceeds to instill an affirmation within us, asserting that we ought to obtain a novel vehicle in due course. Given that our future perpetually eludes us, as we continually reside in the present moment, our coveted aspirations rarely come to fruition.

The human subconscious possesses immense potential for manifestation when one possesses the adeptness to embed positive affirmations within it. Our subconscious mind does not engage in debates with us, but rather accepts and internalizes whatever we consciously instill within it. Upon closer examination, it is apparent that you have neglected to provide a positive affirmation regarding the acquisition of a car within the upcoming years. What actions can be taken to transform this statement into a constructive affirmation? Frequently, I encounter numerous individuals who inquire about the same matter, expressing their inability to achieve prosperity in harnessing the potential of their intellect, physique, and consciousness. I propose the implementation of a straightforward method whereby individuals establish two journals. One journal would be dedicated to recording their aspirations and goals, encompassing their dreams and desired milestones. The other journal would serve the purpose of documenting the actions and endeavors undertaken to attain those aspirations. It is crucial to acknowledge that accomplishments can only be attained through diligent effort, and it is imperative to couple this optimistic mindset with the affirmation that you intend to instill in your Subconscious mind.

Are you familiar with the identity of Thomas Edison? Indeed, he was the renowned scientist responsible for the creation of the light bulb that is still in widespread use in the present era. Prior to his invention of the light bulb, he encountered numerous setbacks. It may come as a surprise to learn that Thomas

Edison endured a thousand unsuccessful attempts before ultimately achieving the invention of the light bulb. This historical anecdote illuminates the considerable effort required to achieve one's desired aspirations in life. I would advise against entertaining any misconceptions and recommend setting attainable objectives for your manifestation. Avoid repeatedly indulging in fantasies about having material possessions and relationships without a concrete plan, as this can create confusion within your subconscious mind. Systematically evaluate the feasibility of each affirmation within the given context, considering them individually. For instance, consider the scenario where you have encountered an exceptionally attractive young woman and are deeply eager to establish a romantic relationship with her. In this situation, it would be prudent to construct a carefully devised and systematic framework of positive declarations, specifically tailored to influence your Subconscious mind. During the initial evening, make a conscious declaration to oneself that "On the following day, I shall confidently present myself to that exquisite lady." Continue to engage in these constructive affirmations, gradually and consistently, until you attain your desired outcome, whether it be finding a life partner, a soul mate, or simply engaging in a brief intimate encounter.

Now consider the case of a luxury car, but this time, rephrase the statement in a positive manner and mentally reiterate it as follows: 'I sincerely value owning a luxury car in my garage, as it allows me to embark on extensive drives with my family and loved ones.' By adopting this approach, instead of framing your statement in the future tense, you have inserted a favorable perception into your subconscious mind, affirming that you will undoubtedly acquire a luxury car within a few months. This way, it becomes deeply ingrained in your subconscious and paves the way for the successful realization of your manifestation. Document the sequential actions you are undertaking in order to acquire a high-end automobile within your personal journal, as I am confident that this diligent record-keeping will also serve as a catalyst for attaining your desired outcome.

Not Mere Existence in the Present Moment

Delving into more profound realms and potentialities. Observing the manifestation of the Law of attraction.

An unsettled mind is akin to a disturbed pond, teeming with incessant ripples. Consciousness can be likened to the act of an individual beholding their own likeness as it is reflected upon the surface of a tranquil pond. As you cast several pebbles into the pond, a moment will arise when your reflection becomes completely obscured, leaving only the sight of expanding ripples. The majority of individuals have come to accept that those undulations constitute their essence or their authentic being. It is only when the turbulence of those ripples subsides, yet the presence of one's self remains intact, that one comprehends the distinction between being the ripples and being the observer of them. One will encounter this phenomenon subsequent to engaging in the yogic exercises discussed in the following chapter, however, mere adherence to the yogic postures alone does not suffice to attain samyukti. And in the event that you are prepared, it is not imperative to engage in yogic postures in order to achieve samyukti.

What does Samyukti Mean?

Samyukti means coherence. This phenomenon is referred to by various names, one of which is infinite intelligence, as designated by Napoleon Hill. Within the law of attraction community, individuals often refer to this concept as "the vortex," coherence, or the essence of the soul. However, in essence, they are all referring to the identical phenomenon. This mental state can be referred to as "samyukti," a term I have coined to denote a state of coherence. This is a quality that can solely be acquired by a consciousness that is unattached to anything other than mindfulness.

Should you hold the belief that you are solely the mind, your consciousness shall be fixated upon it, thereby limiting your perception solely to the mind, excluding any other facets of existence. It is possible for one to perceive themselves as observing the external world, yet in reality, they are merely perceiving their own mental constructs projected through the faculties of their sensory perception and consciousness. Should your consciousness become fixated upon a particular matter, that matter shall manifest as your experienced reality and all other aspects of existence shall be perceived through the filter of that singular matter. The mind is a limited reflection of creation, and relying solely on the mind's perception can offer only a partial understanding. Not everything.

If one has entrenched their consciousness within the realm of the intellect, their sole perception shall be limited to reminiscences of the past or projections of hypothetical futures. Please ascertain, at present, whether you embody the notions of the intellect or assume the role of the observer witnessing the manifestations of said intellect.

There exists an additional compartment within the realm of cognition (distinct from the anatomical brain) that operates autonomously. That component does not pertain to the realm of the psyche, nor is it an incidental result or subject to the influence of the mind or any physical entity. That particular aspect is referred to as consciousness. Consciousness does not have the purpose of ensuring our safety; it is not a survival mechanism intentionally bestowed upon us. It is inherent within all entities; it permeates across all existence. It signifies the state of growth.

What is the Reason Behind Our Inability to Recall all of Our Dreams?

Indeed, awareness constitutes merely a fraction of the comprehensive phenomenon of consciousness. Upon entering the state of slumber, one's perceptual faculties are rendered dormant, yet a vestige endures. That particular entity is not interconnected with the faculties of remembrance, hence its absence from your conscious recollection upon waking. Nonetheless, it remains possible to engage in discourse regarding it due to the existence of an internal element that links energy to consciousness within you. The term "subtle body" refers to the entity which comprises a blend of consciousness and refined energy.

Consider this idea. Resort to thumb sucking as an optional action to undertake, while it is not mandatory, it is encouraged for enhanced comprehension and engagement in the activity. Take note of your current position and consider it while engaging in the habit of thumb-sucking. When you engage in the act of sucking your thumb, do you identify yourself as the thumb? Thumb is "your" body. Are you the individual generating negative pressure with your oral cavity? The oral cavity is also an integral component of one's physique. Do you represent the void or vacuum that has been generated through suction? That vacuum is "awareness". Then what is sucking? It is an endeavor that bears resemblance to the complexities and experiences of life. Sustaining oneself by the act of drawing sustenance from a source can be regarded as the quintessential essence of the human existence. It is not a matter of you, but rather the essence of your existence that is being perceived.

What is experiencing life?

The space. The space is aware. Engaging in this activity has the potential to offer you a glimpse into the realm of enlightenment. In this work of art, all elements exist in a state of unbroken continuity. Existence and non-existence are not discrete entities. Existence can prevail in different subtle forms with a slight mix of non-existence. Indeed, the concept of non-existence has no basis in reality.

This creation exhibits a dualistic nature. One entity can be referred to as pure consciousness, whereas the other can be identified as energy, as you might have deduced. These two do not represent the definitive aspects of creation. They possess the ability to amalgamate and generate an endless array of blends, akin to the manner in which the fusion of black and white delivers boundless variations of gray. Nevertheless, it is not feasible to demarcate the exact point at which consciousness ceases and energy originates.

The subtle body can be defined as an entity possessing a delicate emanation of energy, while being in direct connection with absolute consciousness. It represents a realm of samyukti, where the potential for the extraordinary knows no bounds. The subtle body serves as the singular bridge connecting absolute energy and consciousness.

Inherent energy lacks the capacity to observe or perceive as it lacks consciousness. Pure consciousness can only perceive its own existence, as it is inherently conscious and incapable of observing external entities. Expressed in formal language, the statement could be rephrased as follows: "It poses a considerable challenge to articulate using verbal means, yet these two entities are paradoxically exhibiting a symbiotic relationship, characterized by their mutual independence and coalescence, provoking and shaping one another's manifestations within the intricate structure of creation." In simpler terms, we may refer to it as an infinite value.

Now, the inquiry lies in the manner by which we may gain access to it.

One is not necessarily required to attain absolute consciousness in order to achieve one's desires. However, it is only when one aspires to gain ultimate control over the law of attraction that it becomes imperative to detach oneself from energy. Samyukti refers to a state of mind characterized by complete immersion in pure consciousness, devoid of any external energetic influence. In the state of Samyukti or coherence, one perceives energy in its unadulterated form.

Once awareness attains a state of absolute purity and disengages itself from any manifestation of energy, it relinquishes the notion of self and sheds the illusory facade of control, for awareness is inherently incapable of exerting control. It can only allow. This consciousness of absolute nature possesses infinite intelligence and is aware of every minute detail within the entirety of this creation. It is the principle that transforms the nonexistent into existence and allows energy to manifest in its current form. This location is the repository of comprehensive knowledge about all phenomena in the cosmos.

I have addressed the topic of fictional entities in my literary work titled "The secret path to supernatural" with the purpose of guiding readers towards accessing more ethereal dimensions of existence, on a subconscious level. There undoubtedly exist phenomena that transcend the realms of the conscious, subconscious, and the material.

Do not make the assumption that the physical realm will manifest itself as a separate and distinct facet of existence. This assertion lacks veracity due to the inherent characteristic of reality being characterized as continuous and not discrete. In the event of uncertainty, you can readily ascertain the veracity of this claim by immersing oneself within the realm of pure consciousness. There exist various levels of existence, ranging from absolute nothingness to the state of being. In essence, "physical" reality is not inherently absolute. It represents merely a singular extremity of the absolute spectrum.

Allow us to review the pragmatic measures required to achieve Samyukti.

In the initial phase, we will proceed with the elimination of all fraudulent identities that have been assumed. These identities serve as impediments separating you from establishing a connection with Samyukti. When we perceive ourselves as intelligent individuals, individuals of limited financial means, exceptionally brilliant individuals, prosperous individuals, contented family-oriented individuals, skilled gamers, reserved individuals, outgoing individuals, or sociable individuals, we deceive ourselves with falsehoods, thus diminishing our personal empowerment.

The concepts that the mind associates with its own essence are fiercely safeguarded, as there exists a belief that relinquishing these identities would lead to demise. One effective pragmatic method to relinquish all affiliations involves documenting personal characteristics and preferences on a piece of paper. This exercise encompasses a wide range of aspects including one's preferences, aversions, admiration towards various entities, desired objectives, and the individual one aspires to embody. Compose an autobiographical account outlining the significant aspects of your life. Now, examine each individual identity that your mind has assumed.

Nevertheless, the subconscious mind possesses a superior nature in comparison to the conscious mind, as it encompasses and surpasses the capabilities of the latter. Merely applying conscious effort to contemplate and verbally affirming to oneself that one does not embody these identities will prove ineffectual. It is imperative to engage in a consistent practice of reading aloud the written material and consciously affirming that those aspects do not define your identity. However, it is crucial to recognize that this may not be sufficient. Therefore, I am inclined to offer you a highly effective visualization technique, known as the black bull technique, in a subsequent chapter. This technique will effectively dissolve the untrue notion of self and facilitate an immediate connection with samyukti.

It is imperative to adhere precisely to the techniques as stipulated in the book, given their pronounced efficacy. This denotes that it has the potential to significantly impact your life or induce psychosis with equal ease. If the trajectory of a shuttle rocket's launch is even slightly miscalculated, the resulting deviation over substantial distances would lead to significant directional changes, potentially causing it to miss the moon's vicinity by a considerable margin of at least one thousand kilometers, or perhaps more, unless the rocket is steered by thrusters or closely monitored by supervisors. The entirety of the book is focused on achieving unparalleled samyukti.

The Perception of Phantom Limbs and the State of Pure Consciousness

Keeping that aside. In light of the previous reference to the subtle body, it should be noted that a component of the subtle body exists, known as the energy or pranic body. The pranic body consists of both the aspects of perception that are currently within your awareness and those that you possess the potential to perceive. However, certain dimensions of perception remain inactive. The energy body discerns the presence of other energies by observing the alterations they have induced within its own composition. This energy construct possesses "non-physical appendages", certain ones of which do not reside within the confines of the corporeal form. It is possible that the subtle nature of energy may hinder your ability to perceive it, rendering it undetectable. To illustrate this point, envision attempting to perceive the presence of an antenna positioned on the apex of your head - such a notion would likely be regarded as absurd. There is. Attempt to construct a conceptual appendage resembling a missing limb atop the pinnacle of your cranium, thereby enabling yourself to experience the sensation of a tactile stimulus upon the extremity of said phantom limb. Engaging in this activity will elicit a subtle euphoric sensation. Have you observed individuals of the yogi community maintaining their hair at a longer length, often styled in a manner resembling an antenna?

Furthermore, a comparable experience can be observed by examining the fluid known as mercury, commonly used in thermometers. This substance possesses metaphysical properties that transcend the realm of ordinary sensory perception. Mercury acts as a stimulant to the pineal gland due to its conscious nature or its resemblance to unadulterated consciousness, which manifests and adapts to any form it is presented with. By directing your energy towards this illusionary limb, your vibrational frequencies will significantly elevate, resulting in a state of euphoria. One will experience a profound gravitational force, akin to the exertion of one's vital life energies being extracted forcibly through that antenna. The mind will attain such profound tranquility that it will shift its focus away from the five senses and instead direct it toward the essence of consciousness. The atmosphere would be so void of sound that one might perceive a sensation of mental paralysis. Perhaps while perusing this text, you can envision the emotions that would arise within you. Energy encompasses more than just the physical realm. It pertains to the realm of psychology, lacking physical attributes and encompassing metaphysical aspects. There exists a multitude of amalgamations of energy and consciousness such that if you were to broaden your perspective to the notion of disembodied entities traversing the physical realm, some passing through you, some engaged in their mundane undertakings within their distinct planes of existence, it would be difficult to comprehend such a phenomenon. A tree embodies energy, an idea emanates energy, thought manifests energy, emotion radiates energy, awareness encompasses energy, a dream encapsulates energy, a goal embodies energy, a shape represents energy, geometry is a dimension of energy, everything that you have perceived thus far can be understood as energy. The various manifestations and manifestations of energy may exhibit disparate forms and expressions, yet at its core, everything fundamentally constitutes energy. Energy is the paramount substance of both creation and duality. From the utmost degree of firmness (the materiality of objects) to the utmost degree of refinement, to the point where it dissolves into pure consciousness (which represents the most refined manifestation of energy or the state of absolute energy absence), every entity is simply a particular manifestation of energy. The concept of nothingness does not exist. There exists an omnipresent element in every vicinity, permeating even the most minute particles and vacant expanses, engendering the essence of objecthood. That is consciousness. However, there exist entities that possess consciousness and energy, extending beyond the realm of human beings to encompass non-physical and more subtle entities. It is superfluous, however, enlisting their assistance in actualization can truly provide a significant advantage. These entities exist ubiquitously, and their oscillations are contingent upon the resonance of your own oscillations. It may require a substantial amount of perseverance to cultivate the insight to perceive them, while also recognizing that not all possess an aesthetically pleasing appearance; certain beings possess admirable qualities, yet evoke both dread and awe. For instance, certain entities exhibit a combination of a human physique and a canine countenance, some possess a blend of equal proportions of white and black, whereas others possess facial features of such magnitude that they would not be accommodated by the dimensions of a standard room door. Furthermore, there exists an individual that bears the visage of an elephant along with a humanoid physique.

We prefer not to interfere with any of them. All of these entities represent the cognitive processes of the human intellect. A corporeal entity possesses the capability to fashion or procreate any form of existence, as the human being's endeavors encompass creation across all dimensions. Spanning from the utmost inflexibility to its most delicate manifestation. As previously stated, maintaining good physical hygiene is crucial. However, it is equally important to prioritize mental and emotional hygiene as well. In the event that one's thoughts and emotions are immersed in a state of negativity, the likelihood of experiencing positive and serendipitous outcomes diminishes. In addition, olfactory stimuli exert a significant influence on our oscillatory patterns. The impact of odor on our thoughts and emotions is of such significance that it is imperative to explore this potentiality. If you cook popcorn. The scent it emits is so enticing that it would inspire one to venture out to the cinema. Burning an incense stick will naturally elicit feelings of joy and promote positive thoughts. If at any point you perceive a lack of coherence within your family circumstances or if any of your relatives display symptoms of depression or emotional distress. Attempt to ignite several incense sticks or infuse a small amount of jasmine oil, and observe their ensuing ephemeral radiance. The sense of smell exerts a remarkably substantial impact on our cognitive processes. The presence of a subtle odor reminiscent of a drainage system has the potential to swiftly dampen one's spirits. If an unpleasant odor permeates your home, it is highly likely that the overall atmosphere within is similarly unappealing. Please bear in mind that not all pleasant odors exhibit significantly elevated vibrational frequencies. Consider employing aromatic oils and incense sticks as alternatives to merely masking or concealing unpleasant odors with air fresheners. Ensure that your surroundings remain organized and uphold cleanliness.

If your environment emits unpleasant odors, it is highly likely that your vibrations also possess an unfavorable scent.

A Subconscious Program

The existence of a subliminal algorithm has the capacity to influence our thought processes, emotions, and actions. When one contemplates, experiences emotions, and conducts oneself in a particular manner, a corresponding outcome will be obtained. This outcome may either align with your desired expectations or diverge from them. In instances where individuals fail to achieve their desired outcome, a common tendency among them is to modify their actions or behaviors accordingly. Merely a small proportion of individuals alter their thoughts and emotions. This is the reason why only a limited number of individuals are able to actualize their aspirations and attain prosperity.

In the initial chapter, we have deliberated upon the means of altering your thought processes and emotions. In this instance, we shall delve into the formation of a subliminal program and its potential implications on one's life.

The formation of a subconscious program occurs when we ascribe significance to a particular experience. An event is neutral. The positivity or negativity of the event is contingent upon the significance we attribute to it. A considerable number of individuals remain unaware of the enduring impact that meaning can have on their entire lifespan. Furthermore, we employ the significance as a guide for our thought processes, emotions, and actions.

Have you retained recollection of the lady afflicted by avian feather phobia? During her early childhood, an inexplicable occurrence transpired where a crow managed to enter her living quarters. The crow perched atop her head, emanating a resounding, high-pitched squawk. She was so frightened. The crow endeavored to locate an escape route, inadvertently collided with the walls, resulting in the shedding of its plumage. The young lady perceived a feather as a perilous object. That was the inception of her phobia.

The process of mind programming is structured into three primary intervals known as the Imprint period, ranging from birth to seven years of age, the Modeling period, spanning from seven to fourteen years, and the Socialization period, encompassing the ages of fourteen to twenty-one. Certain experts suggest that the process of mind programming may commence during the gestational stage, in the very early stages of one's development within the womb of their mother. During the developmental period preceding 21 years of age, we acquire knowledge to the best of our abilities. Starting at the age of 21 and beyond, we will apply the knowledge and experiences we have acquired in order to navigate and make the most of our existence.

The formation of a subconscious program ensues from the attribution of significance to a particular experience. The significance ascribed to the event that has a profound effect on one's life, rather than the event in isolation. Any events are neutral. If you ascribe a favorable interpretation to the occurrence, it will assume a positive connotation, and conversely.

The significance ascribed to the event gives rise to differentiation. Hence, it is evident that divergent accomplishments may arise among siblings who share the same familial background and undergo similar life circumstances.

An elder sibling observed frequent parental discord stemming from financial matters. He construed the incident as, "The recurring cause of discord between my parents is primarily financial in nature." Financial instability is the root cause of issues. I hate money. "I have no desire to amass a considerable amount of wealth." As a mature individual, he would either consciously or unconsciously distance himself from the pursuit of material prosperity.

The younger sibling perceived the situation as indicative of financial constraints within the family, attributing this to the modest earnings of their parents. I aspire to accumulate wealth in order to alleviate the distressing sight of my parents contending over financial matters. His subconscious psyche was ingrained with a predisposition for affluence.

The Law Of Detachment

To obtain or attain any objective, it is necessary to relinquish one's attachment to it. This principle is referred to as the Law of Detachment. The principle of the Law of Detachment asserts that to effectively bring your aspirations into reality, it is imperative to maintain a state of detachment from the ultimate result. Releasing attachment does not entail relinquishing our aspirations or wishes; rather, it involves relinquishing our inclination to impose them. Confuse?

Indeed, articulating the concept of detachment, letting go, or surrender, or whichever terminology one prefers to employ, proves to be a rather challenging endeavor. I have consistently emphasized the importance of contemplating and giving due attention to your aspirations, and I must now assert that in order to actualize your aspirations, it is imperative to relinquish any sentimental attachment to them.

Detachment does not imply renouncing our aspirations. Disengagement should not be misconstrued as relinquishing our aspirations to materialize our dreams. Detachment entails freeing ourselves from the bondage of our desires.

Detachment signifies our belief in the inherent goodness of everything. You direct your attention towards your desired outcome, with the expectation of its manifestation. When such an occurrence transpires, one tends to experience a sense of gratitude. In instances where the occurrence does not transpire, one also experiences a sense of gratitude. You still possess aspirations. You have not been deprived of your longings. You still want it. You merely relinquish your attachment to the outcome.

If we maintain an attachment to the desired result, our attention becomes fixated on the unfavorable aspects and we begin to question our capacity to actualize it. The presence of attachment invariably gives rise to insecurity, regardless of its abundance. Insecurity causes unhappiness.

You may possess a fervent longing or ambition.

If you happen to be an enthusiast of Napoleon Hill's notable literary work, Think and Grow Rich, it is likely that you are currently contemplating how the

Law of Detachment appears to be in apparent contradiction with the teachings you have ingrained. In fact, there is a complete absence of contractions. You may possess an intense passion for your aspirations. It is imperative that you do not foster any attachment to the eventual outcome. What is the difference?

I am confident that you possess aspirations that you aim to accomplish in your lifetime. It is your dream. It is your passion. You aspire to realize your ultimate ambition. The dream signifies your fervent longing or intense aspiration.

Have we established a clear understanding up to this point?

Dispassion does not preclude the act of harboring desires. Detachment involves relinquishing one's attachment to the eventual outcome or result. The outcome, which refers to the day when you accomplish your aspiration, lies ahead in the future. It may occur either tomorrow, in the coming year, or in the forthcoming decades. It lies in the future.

Contemplating the future is futile, as one's existence is confined to the present. One may aspire to a promising future, however, in order to secure a more favorable outcome, one must strive to give their utmost effort in the present. In order to attain your aspiration, it is imperative to concentrate on the actions you are capable of undertaking at present.

"Will I achieve it? When can I expect to attain it? What are the steps necessary to accomplish it? What if I am executing the task incorrectly? What steps should be taken in the event that the desired outcome cannot be attained? Do I possess the requisite qualifications for it?"

Detachment entails relinquishing those thoughts. Attachment only creates insecurity. If one maintains an attachment to the outcome, they are likely to experience a prevailing sense of discomfort and may inadvertently manifest negative emotions such as disbelief, fear, anxiety, distrust, pessimism, and apprehension. Unfavorable emotions solely yield outcomes contradictory to the desired objective. Once more, your emotions define your identity.

Direct your attention to the present moment. Direct your attention to your strategic objectives. Direct your attention to the actions you can take to attain them. The outcome, whether you succeed or not, should be of secondary concern. What is crucial at this point is to execute your plan or proceed with taking action. In the absence of a strategic blueprint or a clear misconception of the methods through which one's aspirations can be realized, the only recourse is to persist in leading an ordinary existence and express gratitude for one's present circumstances.

Detachment entails relinquishing control and surrendering to a higher power. Detachment means you go with the flow, but without giving up on your dreams or desires. Human beings make plans, but ultimately, it is fate or a higher power that determines the outcome. Detachment entails the recognition that God incessantly bestows favorable blessings upon you. Irrespective of the outcome, you will experience gratitude, be it in the realization of your aspirations or otherwise. Irrespective of the realization of your aspirations, you will find contentment in your present circumstances.

Detachment implies finding contentment in the realization of any outcomes attained. You determine that any results you have attained are inherently beneficial and can serve as invaluable learning opportunities. Detachment entails finding contentment and a sense of gratitude, even in the absence of attaining one's aspirations.

Attaining Mental And Physical Relaxation Through Mindful Breathing

"Breathe. Let go. And it is imperative to bear in mind that the present moment at hand is the singular instance that can unequivocally be confirmed.

The initial protocol for implementing the practice of manifestation through relaxation involves employing deliberate breathing techniques to attain tranquility in both the physical and mental realms. Let us explore the methodology by which this task may be accomplished.

Regulate Your Nervous System Through Mindful Breathing

The mere process of inhaling and exhaling brings you to a profound state of introspection within your mind and body. The act of respiration serves to firmly connect one's consciousness to the mind. It serves as a method of harmonizing the physical and mental aspects of oneself, forging a connection between these fundamental elements. As a manifestation of inherent processes, it facilitates a profound comprehension of nature's seamless, unfaltering, and awe-inspiring mechanisms.

It is essential for you to cultivate greater awareness of your breathing and actively engage in the process, enabling you to recognize its extraordinary capacity and comprehend the profound value it holds. Through the intentional regulation of your breath, you can gradually alleviate your tensions. This phenomenon occurs as focusing on your breath enables you to rectify rapid breathing patterns and regulate the manner in which you handle inhalation and exhalation. As soon as your respiratory patterns stabilize, feelings of anxiety, nervousness, and stress will begin to dissipate from your body, concurrent with the stabilization of your cortisol levels. Excessive stress plays a significant role in the development of various health concerns, such as hypertension, diabetes, and cardiovascular ailments. Therefore, by effectively managing your stress, you are able to maintain good health as well. Let us ascertain the optimal approach by which one may cultivate a state of serenity and inner calm.

Practicing Conscious Breathing

Various methods exist for engaging in the practice of conscious breathing. Two efficacious and straightforward techniques for conscious respiration that are advisable for individuals who are new to the practice include equal breathing and abdominal breathing.

Sama Vritti, also known as Equal Breathing, serves as a restorative technique that promotes equilibrium within the body, effectively mitigating various manifestations of stress. Commence by deliberately taking a breath, ensuring that you count to four as you do so. Inhale and retain your breath for a duration of four seconds, subsequently exhaling it gradually and evenly as you count to four. It is advisable that you utilize nasal breathing for inhalation and exhalation. Engage in this activity for approximately two to three minutes, and you will experience a heightened sense of tranquility compared to your previous state. Ensure that you establish your intention towards the calming of your nervous system and the reduction of stress. Furthermore, it is imperative that you redirect your attention solely towards the act of respiration, excluding any other distractions. In the event that your thoughts begin to stray, gently redirect your focus to your breath and fixate solely on the pattern and cadence of each respiration. Equal breathing can be performed at any given moment, nonetheless, its optimum efficacy lies in its utilization as a prelude to sleep.

Diaphragmatic Breathing: Diaphragmatic breathing proves to be highly effective in effectively managing and alleviating one's stress. To engage in this exercise, position one hand on your abdomen and the other on your thorax. Presently, engage in deep inhalation through your nostrils, ensuring that your diaphragm fills with an adequate volume of air to expand your lungs, thereafter proceed to exhale via your oral cavity. It is recommended to engage in a practice of taking approximately five to ten deliberate and prolonged breaths per minute. Engage in abdominal breathing exercises for a minimum duration of five minutes initially, gradually increasing it to a maximum of 15 minutes.

Engage in either of these two breathing techniques, or alternatively, practice both methods on alternating days - depending on your preference. It may require a few days for you to gradually regulate your breathing and attune yourself to it. In the near future, you will have the ability to regulate and calm your brainwaves by utilizing controlled breathing techniques. To achieve a heightened state of focus on matters of true importance, it is necessary to deliberately decelerate the brainwaves and frequencies of your cognitive processes.

Five Brainwave Patterns

There exist essentially five brainwave patterns. The beta brainwave pattern exhibits a frequency spectrum spanning from 12Hz to 38Hz, rendering it the brain's most elevated frequency range. It is released during periods of heightened consciousness, tension, stress, or agitation. The subsequent neural activity pattern corresponds to the alpha brainwave, with a frequency spectrum spanning from 8Hz to 12Hz. This electroencephalographic signal is generated during a state of conscious awareness of external stimuli, coupled with a state of mental or physical relaxation. The third brainwave pattern is characterized as the theta brainwave, exhibiting a frequency spectrum spanning from 3Hz to 8Hz. Typically, this brainwave frequency is observed during periods of profound meditation. The delta brainwave, representing the fourth pattern, encompasses frequencies between 0.5Hz and 3Hz. Its occurrence is typically observed during states of profound meditation or dreamless sleep. The infra-low brainwaves, delineating the fifth pattern, exhibit a frequency below 0.5Hz. These waves, characterized by their exceptionally sluggish nature, constitute the cortical rhythms of the brain. Limited information is available concerning these neural oscillations.

By engaging in conscious breathing, one is capable of progressively reducing and soothing the rhythm of their respiratory motions. This facilitates the attainment of a meditative state wherein you are able to tranquilize your brainwaves, transitioning from the beta brainwave pattern into the theta and delta frequencies. As the activity of your brainwaves decelerates, your cognitive processes decelerate proportionately, allowing you to comprehend and identify the thoughts that act as stress catalysts. Once you have the ability to identify thoughts that induce stress, you can effectively rid your mind of them by simply relinquishing those unfavorable thoughts through exhalation.

In order to acquire the skill of manifesting all desired outcomes through peaceful practices, it is imperative to commence by mastering the art of tranquilizing one's thoughts through the utilization of deliberate and unhurried respiration techniques. By implementing the aforementioned principles, you will swiftly attain this objective. Once you have achieved this objective, you will be prepared to proceed to the subsequent stage.

Scientific Benefits

Even if your primary objective for engaging in meditation goes beyond relaxation, it will inevitably yield this outcome. In the 1970s, a doctor and researcher affiliated with Harvard University by the name of Herbert Benson introduced the phrase "relaxation response" in reference to his studies on individuals who engaged in regular transcendental meditation. The relaxation response can be defined as a physiological reaction characterized by a diminishment in the functioning of the sympathetic nervous system, resulting in an involuntary and contrasting bodily response.

Subsequent investigations into the relaxation response have revealed the subsequent advantages:

Deeper relaxation

Less stress

Enhanced sense of overall wellness

Reduced levels of cortisol in the bloodstream

Slow respiratory rates

Less perspiration

Reduced heart rate

Better blood circulation

Lowered blood pressure

Numerous studies, totaling in the thousands, have been conducted to demonstrate the potential influence of meditation on our overall physical and mental well-being. Research has provided evidence to support the effectiveness of meditation, whether in terms of its positive impact on relationships, enhanced concentration, better sleep quality, or alleviation of stress. Despite ongoing research on digital meditation programs, there exists substantiating evidence advocating the utilization of meditation training for diverse outcomes.

Meditation can significantly influence the following aspects in a beneficial manner:

Depression: The University of Oxford conducted a study indicating that engaging in meditation for a duration of eight weeks exhibits the potential to alleviate symptoms associated with depression.

Anxiety: The aforementioned study also highlighted its potential to alleviate symptoms associated with anxiety.

Clinical Cohort: Findings from two limited-scale investigations demonstrated that the practice of meditation exhibited potential for enhancing the quality of life among individuals diagnosed with cancer.

Occupation: The practice of meditation possesses the potential to enhance job contentment, diminish burnout, and alleviate job-related stress.

Self-compassion: A research conducted by medical professionals indicated that the practice of meditation can enhance one's capacity for self-compassion.

Hostility: The practice of meditation has the potential to lead to a reduction in one's propensity to react strongly to negative feedback and exhibit decreased levels of aggression.

Empathy: An additional research inquiry has revealed that individuals who engage in meditation exhibit empathy by willingly relinquishing their seat to someone in need.

Cognitive State: The practice of meditation has the potential to enhance the fundamental constituents of one's cognitive state, encompassing factors such as irritability and happiness.

Emphasis: The act of making choices, directing one's attention, and maintaining focus play integral roles in our day-to-day existence. The practice of meditation can effectively prevent mental distractions and enhance our concentration abilities.

Psychological stress: Numerous studies have provided evidence of the stress-alleviating effects of meditation in diverse contexts.

Meditation may also exert influence on:

Suffering: The practice of meditation can facilitate the alleviation of physical discomfort.

Chronic illness: According to the American Heart Association, the practice of meditation can mitigate the likelihood of developing cardiovascular complications.

Interpersonal Connections: Extensive research has demonstrated the potential of meditation in enhancing interpersonal communication and nurturing romantic partnerships.

Attaining weight loss: The practice of meditation can facilitate the development of beneficial eating habits. This can contribute to weight reduction if one has been diagnosed with obesity or is characterized as overweight.

Slumber: The practice of meditation has been shown to enhance the quality of sleep among individuals struggling with sleep disturbances.

Ongoing research endeavors are currently examining the potential long-term advantages of engaging in regular meditation practices. Meditation has been observed to have beneficial implications for the immune and cognitive functions of individuals. It is important to reiterate that the primary objective of meditation does not lie in acquiring health benefits. The primary objective of meditation does not entail pursuing a specific outcome. It is imperative to maintain a state of pure presence.

When discussing the philosophical principles espoused by Buddha, a pivotal advantage lies in the practice of meditation, which serves to emancipate the mind from entangling itself with elements beyond its realm of control, such as internal emotions or external circumstances. An individual who has attained liberation will abstain from indulging in their desires and refraining from attaching themselves to temporal experiences in order to cultivate internal balance and a serene state of mind.

Nine Challenges to Conquer

Meditation serves as a cognitive workout for our minds. Through the practice of meditation, individuals can cultivate and strengthen specific neural regions, thereby initiating a process of neuroplasticity that heightens faculties like cognitive reasoning and concentration, while concurrently diminishing afflictions such as stress and anxiety. This implies that it is conceivable to modify the brain in manners that are more advantageous and possess greater permanence.

Meditation serves as a method for cultivating our mental faculties akin to the way we develop our physical abilities. There exists a plethora of diverse meditation practices, and you may be pondering the means by which you can acquire the knowledge to engage in them.

In the realm of Buddhist traditions, 'meditation' holds a synonymous meaning to the term 'sports' within our own cultural lexicon. It encompasses a range of diverse activities, rather than being limited to a singular endeavor. Various practices necessitate distinct skill sets. Distinct practices demand diverse skill requirements. Diverse practices call for varying skillsets.

For an individual who is in the initial stages of learning meditation, it can pose significant challenges to sit for extended periods and engage in sustained contemplation or achieve a state of mind devoid of thoughts. An effective method to commence the practice of meditation is by directing your attention to the rhythm of your breath. The prevailing method typically involves the focus of attention.

In the initial stages of engaging in meditation, it is common for the mind to lack stability. Our minds will inherently seek external assistance. Our cognitive processes are susceptible to the impact of our emotional states. As we progress on this journey, the implementation of meditation can contribute to its enhancement. Buddha imparted teachings on various forms of meditation, which we shall delve into shortly. Let us examine the numerous challenges one may encounter when acquiring the skill of meditation and explore potential strategies to overcome them.

The aforementioned impediments encompass indulgence in fantasies, reminiscing over past experiences, experiencing a sense of emptiness, undergo mental deterioration, lacking comprehension of meditation, experiencing fatigue and drowsiness, being excessively occupied, lacking self-discipline, and lacking motivation. Let us thoroughly examine these issues and determine strategies to surmount them.

Fantasizing on Things

Occasionally, we find ourselves becoming preoccupied with indulging in whimsical thoughts. This is a frequently encountered challenge. One could express the same idea in a formal tone as follows: "It is my desire to attain a millionaire status, and I possess the necessary qualities and capabilities to accomplish this goal. Through the practice of meditation, one can successfully align their thoughts and cultivate a well-defined course of action." This is fine. Engaging in this fantasy without conscious awareness precludes the practice of meditation. The practice of meditation has the potential to enhance cognitive clarity and attune one's receptiveness to their inner thoughts and guidance.

Past Impressions

Meditation proves to be an effective method in mitigating the lingering imprints of our past experiences. During the practice of meditation, it is possible that the occurrence of past memories or incidents may give rise to difficulties or challenges. The practice of meditation has the capacity to cleanse both our minds and bodies. We must address these issues through the application of practices centered around empathy and serenity.

Feeling Empty

During the process of meditation, one may experience a state of mental emptiness or a complete absence of thoughts. One may have attempted meditation and reflected upon it by acknowledging, "That experience was highly unpleasant." Nothing matters. There is a lack of justification for anything. I experienced a sense of powerlessness, which can be attributed to the improper implementation of meditation techniques. Meditation is believed to foster a sense of interconnectedness with the entirety of existence.

Mental Destruction

While you are meditating, there will be many thoughts about your future, past, responsibilities, duties, dislikes, likes, depression, and anger. It is imperative to distance yourself from these thoughts. Simply observe the thoughts and proceed. Your respiration has the potential to facilitate the release of these thoughts from your cognitive faculties.

Lacking a comprehensive grasp of meditation.

Any of our five senses has the potential to serve as a source of distraction during the practice of meditation. These sensory perceptions serve as the access points to previous recollections, cognitions, and affective states. The practice of meditation possesses the potential to refine these faculties, thus contributing to the improvement of the world. We engage in the practice of meditation not as a means to detach ourselves from society, but as a means to introspect, discover our true selves, and gain a deeper understanding of our surroundings. Once one's vision is restored, it is imperative to take decisive action. Through the practice of meditation, one can ascertain the necessary course of action to provide assistance.

Experiencing Fatigue and Drowsiness

Meditation facilitates the cultivation of introspection and appreciation for our inner essence and aesthetics. The purpose is to embody absolute mindfulness in each and every moment. When engaging in the practice of meditation, it is imperative to channel our energy towards fostering a heightened state of awareness. Inadequate sleep practices are the primary cause of fatigue experienced. It is necessary to align your daily routine in accordance with your waking and sleeping patterns. Engaging in a regular yoga practice can enhance the functioning of the circulatory system, musculature, pulmonary system, and cardiovascular system. Consume nourishing food and ensure proper hydration. Ensure you obtain ample rest following an arduous day at the office. This can aid in the recuperation of your physical well-being.

Too Busy

To engage in meditation, one must exert dedication and allocate a significant amount of time. If one's daily routine is excessively demanding, it may impact the ability to wholeheartedly engage with the metaphysical plane. The crux of meditation lies in being conscious and attentive in every action we undertake, while approaching it with meticulousness and genuine affection.

No Self-Discipline

Without possessing a certain degree of self-discipline, the practice of meditation will prove unattainable. Acquiring self-discipline will provide individuals with liberation from feelings of anxiety, depression, and guilt. It is essential that you incorporate meditation into your daily regimen. Exercising self-discipline is essential for establishing new habits, which in turn facilitates the attainment of your objectives. It is essential that you establish clear priorities and develop a structured schedule for your tasks. Establishing a consistent evening routine and adhering to a regular wake-up schedule can significantly contribute to the cultivation of self-discipline. It is imperative to consistently allocate time for daily meditation. It is viable to seamlessly integrate yoga and meditation.

No Motivation
This may be attributed to a lack of comprehensive comprehension regarding the myriad benefits that can be derived from engaging in meditation. Meditation does not possess any affiliations with religious or spiritual

practices. It primarily pertains to activities that are centered around life. The practice of meditation has the potential to enhance both your physical well-being and emotional contentment. It is capable of enhancing cognitive acuity, promoting relaxation, and facilitating cognitive organization.

Types of Meditation

Meditation provides individuals with an opportunity to unwind and enhance their perception in a society rife with tension that tends to desensitize our faculties. According to research findings, meditation can provide a multitude of benefits beyond merely alleviating stress.

Various forms of meditation have been developed by mental health professionals, spiritual leaders, and educators. This implies that there will be a suitable form for the majority of individuals, irrespective of their lifestyle or personality.

For individuals who engage in the practice of meditation, it affords them an opportunity to enhance their overall well-being in conjunction with their emotional and mental well-being. There exists no definitive correct or incorrect approach to the practice of meditation. This indicates that you evaluate and examine the various options available until you identify the one that is most effective for you.

Here are some notable aspects regarding the different types of meditation:

It is entirely acceptable to integrate or experiment with diverse methodologies until you discover the one that best suits your needs.

Various individuals who instruct meditation possess divergent perspectives regarding the frequency at which one ought to engage in this practice.

Within each category of meditation, there exist various subcategories that one can engage in and explore.

Presented herewith are a selection of exemplary techniques for engaging in meditation:

Concentration Meditation

This particular form of meditation entails directing your attention towards a single object or concept. Possible alternative phrasing in a formal tone: - This could involve focusing on one's breath, engaging in the repetition of a sacred phrase, attentively listening to a recurring sound produced by a gong, fixing one's gaze upon the steady flame of a candle, or using mala beads for counting purposes. Due to the inherent difficulty in maintaining mental focus, individuals who are new to meditation may opt to commence their practice by meditating for a mere five minutes, gradually extending the duration over time.

Within this form of meditation, one simply redirects their consciousness back to the designated focal point whenever they become aware of their thoughts straying. Rather than pursuing each thought, you simply release them. This procedure enhances your capacity to focus.

Mindfulness Meditation

This particular form of meditation promotes the cultivation of mindfulness and heightened awareness. Rather than allowing concerns about the future or fixation on the past to consume you, mindfulness meditation promotes the cultivation of present-moment awareness. Exercising non-judgment is imperative for this particular form of meditation. Rather than dwelling on the annoyance caused by a lengthy wait, it is advisable to simply acknowledge the duration without passing judgment upon it.

This particular form of meditation can be practiced in any location. In the event of a queue forming at the checkout counter of the grocery store, one could simply observe and make mental notes of the surrounding environment. This encompasses any aromas, auditory stimuli, and visual elements that you may encounter.

Mindfulness is an intrinsic component of the majority of meditation practices. Developing mindfulness of one's breath promotes the observation of one's respiration. Progressive relaxation techniques will facilitate heightened awareness of any tension present within the body. Given that mindfulness permeates various modalities of meditation, it has been subject to extensive investigation.

Extensive research substantiates the notion that the practice of mindfulness has the potential to:

Enhance contentment in interpersonal connections.

Mitigates emotional and impulsive responses.

Improves memory

Improves focus

Prevents you from dwelling on negative emotions.

There is compelling evidence to suggest that the practice of mindfulness may have a positive impact on one's overall health and well-being. A scholarly investigation conducted on African-American males suffering from chronic kidney disease revealed a noteworthy decrease in their blood pressure levels upon incorporating mindfulness meditation into their routine.

By engaging in this particular form of meditation, you will have the opportunity to observe the manner in which your emotions and thoughts unfold in predetermined sequences. Over time, one's discernment of the inclination to evaluate an encounter as disagreeable, agreeable, negative, or positive will increase. With regular practice, you will cultivate an internal equilibrium.

In certain schools of meditation, practitioners will engage in the amalgamation of mindfulness and concentration techniques. The majority of academic fields necessitate the act of maintaining one's composure. It all depends on the teacher.

Transcendental Meditation

This form of meditation constitutes a spiritual practice wherein one assumes a seated posture and engages in gradual, deliberate breathing techniques. The primary objective is to surpass or transcend one's existing state of existence.

Throughout the meditation practice, the emphasis will be placed on directing your attention towards a chosen word or mantra. Your instructor will determine the most suitable mantra considering various criteria. Several of these factors encompass elements such as the timing of the teacher's professional development and the specific year of your birth.

An alternative method affords you the opportunity to select your own mantra. This iteration can be classified as modern; however, it does not possess the attributes of transcendental meditation, despite its outward similarities. During the practice of meditation, it is within your discretion to opt for affirmations such as: "I harbor no fear towards arachnids."

Individuals who have engaged in this particular form of meditation have provided accounts of experiencing enhanced mindfulness capabilities, as well as attaining heightened states of spirituality.

Progressive Relaxation

This particular form of meditation is referred to as body scan meditation. It prompts you to conduct a thorough examination of your body to identify areas of tension. The primary objective is to discern the presence of tension and subsequently alleviate it.

In the course of this meditation session, you shall initiate the process at one extremity of your physique and proceed systematically through every part of your body. It would be advisable to commence with your feet and proceed sequentially upwards.

There exist certain variations of meditation techniques that involve intentional muscle tension followed by subsequent relaxation. Alternative: "Alternative perspectives propose envisioning a wave gently cascading over your physique, effectively soothing and relieving any built-up tension."

Utilizing progressive relaxation techniques may facilitate a state of relaxation and tranquility. It has the potential to mitigate certain forms of persistent pain. Given its ability to induce gradual and consistent relaxation of the body, this particular form of meditation may serve as a viable aid in facilitating improved sleep quality.

Kundalini Yoga

This practice involves incorporating movements, mantras, and deep breathing to create an active form of meditation. It is imperative to enlist the assistance of an instructor in order to accomplish this task. One could acquire knowledge of the mantras and positions within the confines of their own residence.

This is analogous to other variants of yoga; the practice of kundalini has the potential to alleviate discomfort and enhance one's physical prowess. This could potentially enhance your psychological well-being by mitigating symptoms associated with depression and anxiety.

A research conducted in 2008 concerning veterans suffering from persistent lower back pain revealed that the practice of yoga yielded positive outcomes, including an enhancement in their mental well-being, heightened levels of energy, and alleviation of pain.

Breathing Awareness Meditation

This is a form of mindfulness practice that promotes heightened awareness and focus on one's breath. You will engage in deliberate diaphragmatic breathing while simultaneously practicing breath counting or directing one's attention solely towards the breath. Your objective should solely revolve around directing your attention towards your breath while disregarding any other thoughts that arise.

Furthermore, this practice can be classified as a variant of mindfulness meditation. It provides a majority of the aforementioned advantages typically associated with the practice of mindfulness. These benefits encompass heightened emotional adaptability, enhanced focus, and diminished levels of anxiety.